LIFE AFTER
COVID

A Story of Perseverance

Michael Salvatore Jr
with Kameron Williams

For my parents, who taught me how to persevere, and for God, who gave me the opportunity to do so.

"I am hurt, but I am not slain; I'll lay me down and bleed awhile, and then I'll rise and fight again."

—*The Ballad of Sir Andrew Barton*

CONTENTS

AUTHOR'S NOTE

I have heard stories of would-be authors who write their first book, hoping to reach the bestseller lists and make it big; tales of disheveled men hunched over laptops in their mother's basement, with dreams of writing the one-in-a-million book that's going to make them rich; and others who haven't had a job in years while they mooch off their girlfriends, all because they've been working on the one manuscript that would change everything. But these stories are not *my* story. I did not write this book for money or fame, but rather to give people a glimpse into my life over the last four years. To say it has been a wild ride is a severe understatement.

If even one person is encouraged by reading about my trials, perhaps finding themselves in their own impossible situation, this book's purpose will have been fulfilled. I do not share my story to garner pity or dwell on suffering and despair. I share it to offer an example of how to face life's twists and turns. We all have a story—some more difficult than others. I know my life could have been much worse. When I look at others who have faced even greater challenges, I thank

God that wasn't my path. I feel deep compassion for their pain, anguish, and sorrow. No one should have to go through that—but sadly, many do. I keep them in my prayers and hope they find relief. No matter how hard things get, there's always someone out there carrying an even heavier burden. So, rise and fight against adversity the best you can.

CHAPTER ONE

April 2022

Not many people go to sleep and wake up four months later. But there I was, ears screaming, eyes only detecting light and dark, and with a warped sense of taste, touch, and smell. My body wouldn't respond to any movement I asked of it, and I was unable to speak a word. Coffee smelled and tasted like pepper—and still does to this day. Can you imagine a cup of steaming hot black coffee tasting like pepper? Or a refreshing cold brew with a splash of cream—and pepper? Or a tasty latte, except it's not tasty at all because it tastes like…yeah, pepper? The coffee catastrophe aside, I had other problems.

Waking up from a coma is not like in the movies. There was no collective "Hey, look, Mike's back!" exclamation from my family and friends, followed by copious hugs and warm words, and then picking up right where I left off—as if I had simply paused and then unpaused my life. Coming out of unconsciousness was like coming out of one darkness and plunging into another, with me wondering where I was, how I got there, and what date it was. I kept trying to move, but couldn't. Trying to see and hear, but couldn't. My mind raced as I contemplated this dreadful new state of being.

Is this what life is going to be like from now on?

As hopeless as the thought was, I couldn't help but consider it. There was an unmistakable feeling of pressure—questions I had that weren't being answered, faculties of my body that I hadn't regained, and an unknown path ahead that I envisioned as being terrible and difficult. When nurses came in to clean me, my body felt numb and completely out of my control as they moved my limbs here and there to get me washed. The miserable anticipation of what was to come weighed me down. And, dwelling on the dark future ahead of me, I reflected on my recent past. While the nothingness I had come from was hazy and unclear, at least there had been a complete lack of expectations, obligations, and discomfort. There had been peace. No aches, pains, or worries. Just being. And now...now there was this.

They should've just let me die.

My senses of vision and hearing returned gradually in a torpor of blurs and garbled noise. It was like I was trapped underwater, looking up at a shimmering light glowing beyond the surface, and hearing the unintelligible murmurs of people speaking there. I struggled to hear more of the sounds around me, focusing on each slurred word, the conversations becoming clearer piece by piece.

"The patient...vision...hearing..." I could hear a doctor say.

Good! I thought. *I'm understanding more words.*

"Based on...his mental acuity is..." the doctor continued in muffled sound, the room around me a haze of muted echoes and the same tremulous light.

Good, good, good.

"He'll be bedridden for the rest of his life…" The words crystallized.

No, not good at all….

More fear crept in, slowly at first, as I lifted my feeble hand and felt around. I narrowed my eyes and tried to focus, but what I saw only brought more fear and disbelief. The arm I was trying to move was not the limb I had known it to be, but a withered and gnarled appendage with frail fingers curled inward from disuse. I moved it up toward my neck and face, and it brushed against plastic tubing. One of these tubes went directly into my neck, and the other into my nose.

What's this?

The more my vision returned, the more I examined myself, the more horrified I was. I was basically a skeleton—only skin and bones—more emaciated and frailer than anybody I had ever seen. As my weak eyes gazed down at my unrecognizable body, a strange terror gripped me. That couldn't be me, I thought. Only in some twisted nightmare was I the man lying in this hospital bed. So, I waited there in some hopeful, naïve anticipation—waiting to awaken from this dreadful dream. The problem was, I was already awake, and this was reality.

Days passed, and although my faculties were returning, they were far from back to normal. The first time I tried to call for help, thumbing the call button on my bed railing, I found I didn't have the strength to push it. And so, I improvised, lifting my fist and knocking the knuckles of my now deformed-looking fingers against the bed rail. If I did that right as someone was walking by, they heard it and came to assist me.

Since I could now see a little, hear a little, and move a little, I decided it was time to try speaking. This was a tall order with a trach still attached, but I found, after some experimentation, that I could manage a few words if I exhaled hard while speaking. But I could only get out three or four words before collapsing with exhaustion. Between listening to the doctors and nurses and examining myself as my senses continued to return, I learned several things—none of them encouraging. I had been in a coma for four months. I'd had a tracheotomy and was eating through a feeding tube, hence the tubing running into my neck and nose. I had lost eighty pounds, or about 35% of my body weight. I'd had a stroke. I had died twice while I was comatose. I had blood clots in my lungs and legs, an abscess, and a pressure wound on my butt.

This can't happen—not now—I just got engaged!

But it was more than that. Being in this crippled, near-helpless state went against every part of who I was as a person. The Roman poet Juvenal said that one should have *mens sana in corpore sano*—"a sound mind in a sound body"— and before this whole ordeal, I embodied that. I was a gym rat who could squat, bench, and curl 525, 405, and 235 lbs., respectively, and I had a bachelor's degree, two masters, and a Ph.D. with 25 certifications and 45 years of experience in the pharmaceutical industry. So, as you might imagine, my intellect and fitness were very important to me.

I soon learned that I was in the 1% of people who became debilitatingly sick from COVID-19 and survived. And of that 1%, only 1% recovered to a semblance of their previous life. Of course, the goal was then to become a member of the 1% of the 1%.

I thought about my multiple degrees, certifications, and other accomplishments—and the hard work it took to achieve them. I pondered on my previous level of strength and fitness, which now seemed reduced to zero. Was it all for naught? Again, I thought about how I had gotten engaged in the winter right before I caught COVID. At 66, it was something I never thought I'd do again. Then, the only thing I could think about was fixing all of this. I needed to get back to myself. My highly educated, knowledgeable, and competent self. I needed to be able to get things done like I always did. I needed to be able to take care of my fiancée.

And then my favorite quote passed through my mind like an anthem of hope: "I am hurt, but I am not slain; I'll lay me down and bleed awhile, and then I'll rise and fight again." This line is linked to Sir Andrew Barton, a Scottish privateer (or pirate, depending on one's perspective) who sailed under the Scottish crown in the early 16th century. Most sources trace it to a later ballad recounting his final battle in 1511, although it is sometimes attributed to John Dryden or others. Despite the historical ambiguity of very old ballads, its connection to Barton is well-documented. Regardless of its origin, I knew I must heed its message.

I must rise and fight again.

CHAPTER TWO

B ut let's go back and give you some context for all of this. The year is 2020, and I don't need to tell you what's happening. The public is wearing masks, and a great number of people are convinced toilet paper will run out and are wiping it (pun intended) from the shelves of grocery stores to stockpile in their homes. The COVID-19 pandemic is in full swing.

COVID-19 is caused by the SARS-CoV-2 virus, which belongs to the coronavirus family (*Coronaviridae*). The name "coronavirus" comes from its structure, namely spike proteins that resemble a crown (corona means "crown" in Latin), which help it bind to human cells. This novel coronavirus is part of a larger group of viruses that also includes SARS, MERS, and some common cold viruses.

The CDC confirmed the first case of COVID-19 infection in the United States on January 20th, 2020, with samples taken from a man in Washington State who had recently traveled from Wuhan, China. This new strain was identified in China during December 2019 when hundreds of Chinese fell ill. By late February, it had been detected in several states, and by March it had surged through multiple major cities, prompting lockdowns and travel restrictions. The World Health Organization (WHO) officially declared it a pandemic on March 11th, 2020, and by then the virus had spread to over 100 countries with thousands of cases worldwide.

When the pandemic struck, my fiancée, who was then living in New York, moved in with me in New Jersey. We were very careful with exposure and quite meticulous in our attempts at preventing infection. We wore masks, of course, washed our hands frequently, isolated, and sprayed our deliveries with disinfectant. My fiancée was having work done to her apartment back in New York, and it shocked us both to hear that one of the workers had died from COVID-19. Not long after, my cousin contracted the virus and also passed from it.

Sometimes it's hard to rationalize what you hearing on the news when you don't see it happen around you with your own eyes or hear about it from people you actually know. But when people around you start getting sick—or even dying—it feels as real as something you can reach out and touch, and you consider that life might be different from then on. I had no idea just how different it would be.

My professional background in pharmaceuticals is in drug discovery and development, so I knew that isolation, therapy, and prevention were the keys to health during such a challenging time. I also knew that it should take about 12 years to bring a drug to market, not 18 months. What's more, I could find no compelling data that supported the vaccine's efficacy. I have a Ph.D. in microbiology and almost half a century's worth of experience in Big Pharma, and these were concerns I could not ignore. Finally, after my fiancée and I got tested for allergies to the vaccine's components and were both found to be allergic, the decision to not get vaccinated was a simple one. We lived without infection for two years, but when COVID-19 did come knocking, it came for more than one of us.

My fiancée, her mother, and I all contracted COVID at the same time. We all got the monoclonal antibodies, and I am happy to say that the therapy was quite effective for my fiancée and her mother. For me, however, it was not.

I spent the next five days in bed with fever, GI issues, sweating, and chills. My breathing became progressively worse until every breath was a gasping wheeze, and I was so fatigued I thought I might just topple over. I took an Uber to Mount Sinai Hospital in midtown, and as I passed the Lincoln Center, I feared that it might be the last time I ever saw it.

Once I got checked into the emergency room, I noticed, strangely enough, that there were no other patients there. They checked my oxygen level, and when I saw the eyes of the triage nurse widen to the whites, my heart dropped. My level was 84%. To put things into perspective, the normal range is between 95% and 100%. Anything below 90% is concerning, and 84% is downright terrible. It indicates severe hypoxia—low oxygen in the blood—and it was a critical sign that my brain and body weren't getting enough oxygen.

I was put in an isolation room and given a blanket. I needed that blanket too, that room was freezing. I could've used a few blankets. I huddled there under one thin blanket, shivering as I grew colder and dizzier, my vision waning and my head feeling heavy. Then, I was out.

Much the opposite of the cold I felt before I went out, I awoke feeling so warm I thought the room might've been on fire. So warm I couldn't breathe, only gasp and choke on hot, stuffy air. It didn't occur to me that my own body was the problem rather than the room being set at the wrong temperature. That is, until my series of battles with the nurses about how cool the room was. When they left, I would turn the heat down. Then, they would sneak in while I was dozing and turn it back up. When I noticed, I would turn it down again. And on and on it went.

I noticed that patients in the rooms adjacent to mine were recovering and going home. And each time someone was discharged, I thought hopefully, or maybe foolishly, that I might be next. But I never was. I was hooked up to oxygen, tired all the time, and I knew my situation was bad. I was reminded of this when my fiancée came to visit me. I could tell by her face alone that I looked just as I felt—like a shell of my former self. She didn't want to leave, and I knew it was even worse than I thought.

It wasn't long before everything became a struggle—even something as simple as going to the bathroom. I had a cannula for oxygen, but the tube was too short and wouldn't reach the restroom. So, I had to take it off, rush to the bathroom, and finish as fast as I could. Then I had to stagger back to the bed quickly and unsteadily for my oxygen. When lying down, it felt like I had a huge weight on my chest. They ran CAT scans, X-rays, and bloodwork throughout the weekend. I was placed on a blood thinner, but the kicker here was that it had to be injected—and that was very painful. It left black and blue marks on my abdomen with every injection.

And that wasn't all, I consistently heard "code red" in the rooms next to mine, which meant someone had died. I didn't want to think—didn't dare to—that I might be next.

One night, I sneezed and blew a blood vessel in my nose. Who knew a little "hachoo" could puncture a vein? The blood just wouldn't stop. I drenched three hand towels, and all the sprays and alum they used were for naught. Finally, they put in an inflatable plug, and it was in there for four days. When they removed it, excess blood splattered down all over me. I was a bloody mess.

But I didn't have time to worry about the blood soiling my hospital gown. The doctors came in and informed me that I was critical, and I went to the ICU. Another sedative. More fatigue. Dizziness. My vision turning to dwindling dark circles. And then nothing.

I awoke four months later in a totally different hospital. Apparently, I had been moved from New York City to New Jersey into a halfway house.

Waking up should always be a good thing. The light in your eyes and breath in your lungs means you're alive. A promise of time left in the world. The hope of future joy. Waking up should always be good. Some people don't wake up.

But waking up to find yourself in a state worse off than when you went to sleep isn't good at all. And being given more and more information about the sorry state you're in feels like a never-ending fall into a dark and bottomless pit. Just when you think it can't get worse, it does, and you fall even lower. And when you think, "At some point, I have to hit the ground," you find that you are mistaken, and you keep on falling.

I had awoken from the complete unknown, as if I had skipped through time and space, and all I wanted to hear was my fiancée's voice. That was the only thing that would comfort me. I viewed her as my rock, someone who would tell me that everything would be okay. Being in a coma seemed like it was a flash, a micro-second in my life. Why couldn't the arrival of my fiancée come just as quickly? I just lay there and waited. It seemed like an eternity.

When my fiancée first came in, I still couldn't see well, and I was spared the look on her face when she saw me that I would come to know later—both the facial expression itself and the reason for it. Though my hearing wasn't a hundred percent, either, I could hear the happiness and relief in her voice as she spoke to me. But there was something else. I heard fear.

This wasn't fear that I was going to die or something—the concern of some inevitable doom falling upon me, no, this was more subtle. It was reticence, holding back, the apprehension of telling me about something that had already happened.

Once I noticed she was holding back, I simply asked her, "What happened?"

But she didn't give me a straight answer, and it was my first clue that things were bad. Really bad. "Just…check your file," she told me.

As you can imagine, that wasn't very encouraging. I knew I had been placed in a coma, but what else could've happened while I was out? Then I suffered with this lack of information, racking my brain for possibilities. Thankfully, I didn't have to wonder for long. The nurses came in, and I was able to get some answers.

This is when I found out I was in the 1% of people who got as sick as I did from COVID but didn't die from it. I also learned about my stroke and a host of other issues. When I breathed, and especially when I coughed, I felt a really bad pain in my chest. I was told it was a side-effect of pneumonia. That's right, on top of everything else, I had contracted pneumonia. "Your lungs aren't working efficiently enough to keep in oxygen," a nurse told me as she pointed to the cannula in my nose. I had to be supplemented with oxygen from January until mid-May.

Our conversations made sense now. I had had a stroke on the left side of my brain, which explained the dizziness when I rolled and the lack of movement on my right side. This was unfortunate because I was right-side dominant. The physical therapist also came in and gave me her evaluation and confirmed why I had a lack of movement on my right side.

"Anything else?" I asked the nurse, not actually expecting that there might be more.

"Well," she said, "You coded." She didn't need to tell me that was hospital-speak for dying, and I could see the gravity in her eyes.

That's right, I had died. And twice at that.

I began to contemplate this, and I then dredged up memories from my coma. In retrospect, I had both dreams and visions, and I am now able to differentiate between them. My dreams were as any dream, but my visions all ended with a bright white light, and then I remembered another vision. I could vividly recall a wonderful place with no aches, pains, or worries—a bitter contrast to my new reality. I was angry I was back here—in reality—with pain and weakness and sorrow. Then I thought of how unlikely it was that I was even alive. I guess it hadn't been my time and God had sent me back for some reason.

Since all this happened, I have spoken to several people who went through similar circumstances. They all said the same thing: "It was so peaceful I wish I could've stayed, and I was pissed to be back." I pondered it all for some time, and my scientific take is when you are conscious and you die, you are aware and you float, hover, and witness what is going on. Some people who have died talk about seeing themselves hovering as doctors worked on them. When the doctors made rounds the next day, these people would introduce themselves and relate what they saw and what the doctors had said. For me, I was in a coma and not cognizant of my surroundings. I just passed without a whimper or sound.

In retrospect, I guess God works in his own time and guides us on our journey. I am sure my purpose for being back will become clear to me sometime in the future, and if not, just being alive is enough! Whatever it is, I am all in. The other possibility is that I come from an Italian family from Newark, New Jersey, and we can be very difficult at best. My dad and uncle are now in heaven, and perhaps, as in life, they are quite a handful up there. Maybe God figured two Salvatores were enough and couldn't handle a third. Send Mike back!

I was in awe and confused—but mostly confused. I would often close my eyes and try to sift through the memories of my time being comatose. Strange memories. Enchanting memories. I saw myself, but it wasn't myself. Or it was me, but…different. Different versions of myself in different places, doing a variety of things and talking to a motley assortment of people in a language I didn't understand.

I learned that the first time I died, I flatlined for two minutes. And the second time for three, both in the same day. I had to wonder if I had these dreams and visions the entire time I was in a coma or just when I died. If the latter, a lot sure can happen in five minutes. For I was in Malaysia—India—Kentucky—various parts of New Jersey—New York City—New England—Russia—and even the Arctic.

I suppose that in a way, after everything that had happened, I was grateful for my entire existence—both in the visions I could partly recall and in reality. After everything, I was just happy to *be*— in this body, in this life, in this brutal, broken miracle . I was happy to be anywhere and everywhere. But it put me on a mission to remember and make sense of everything I saw while I was either dead or comatose.

I didn't have the experience of my soul leaving my body, hovering over myself and looking down upon me. No, I saw distinct images and scenes playing through my mind's eye like a film.

CHAPTER THREE

The first scene that surfaced in my dreams was of me in a glass room. The transparent walls were like the floor-to-ceiling windows you see in fancy high-rise apartments. But this room did not speak of luxury, and through those window walls, I could see myself lying in bed, a woman at my side attending me. In hindsight, I'm quite sure the room represented the ICU, and the woman was my nurse. I had this interactive device that kept me amused, and I also dreamt that I had an office in NYC that I shared with another doctor. I sometimes slept there, and an old neighbor would drop by to visit. In addition, I saw that my fiancé had an apartment on the second floor of a building that sold dresses. She would keep the light on so I could always find my way back to her. I'd park my Jaguar in front of the building.

Speaking of my fiancée, there was one who appeared constantly in my dreams and visions.

While the images of her are unclear in my memory, like looking through foggy glasses, there was something familiar about her. She was always by my side throughout my journey. I wonder if it was her.

I also dreamed that my Aunt Nancy was with me, looking the same as I always remembered her, a woolen coat covering her tiny four-foot-three frame. She wore the same yellow hand-kerchief tied around her neck, the same fur-lined black boots. She was always carrying around a plastic bag, and there wasn't a single person she didn't befriend. I took care of her for over twenty years, and it was so nice to see her again, even if it was only in my dreams.

My Aunt Nancy was one of eight children in the first gen-eration of her family born in Newark, New Jersey. Her father passed when she was one, leaving behind a wife and seven other children. Needless to say, they were very poor. Aunt Nancy had a fourth-grade education and worked in ware-houses and kitchens her entire life. She never complained—she simply lived and was happy. She was all of 51 inches tall and never threw anything out. Depression babies did that. Collections of pop tops, used aluminum foil, plastic tops, elastic bands, plastic bags, and disposable containers were her specialty. She also loved animals, never married, and had a strong sense of family. Because of her mental acuity and small stature, she always lived with someone who could take care of her. The onus of that fell on me when my mom passed away. I cared for her for over twenty years.

In my dreams, I would see Aunt Nancy walking towards me from a distance with a stuffed plastic bag in her hand. She didn't bother to stop and say hello, as if she knew I was already aware of her presence and therefore didn't need to. Like I had just stopped in for a visit. Her plastic bag full of junk was a familiar sight. She, like many other women from Newark, would hide their purses in the bottom of plastic bags and pile stuff on top. You were less likely to get robbed that way. Aunt Nancy lived with me and my dad, who I also took care of for over 20 years. I took her shopping, made sure she kept doctor's appointments, and we would watch TV together. She loved her TV, especially science fiction movies and shows. Most of all, she loved coffee and sweets. She always tried to cook—rarely with success—but we made it work. She could bake up a storm, though! I could never figure out how she did it.

In one dream concerning her, I saw an interesting scene. She was living in an apartment in a local port town. The space had no windows, so it must've been a basement apartment, and there were several cats with her. They purred, nuzzled against her, and meowed for food. Seeing her in this quiet, parallel life was strangely comforting. She seemed at peace, and I felt at peace watching her.

The next set of images flashing through my memory was me in Malaysia. I was a young man, was married, and had three kids. My wife was a nurse, and I drove her to work with our kids in the backseat. I remember the countryside, as beautiful as ever, and the elephants playing in the water, spraying each other with their trunks. I wore a loose tunic and spoke the local language—though I couldn't tell you what I said. I remember my wife kissing me before she went to work and the kids giving her hugs. There was a flash of light, and I was somewhere else.

This time, I was a young boy whose parents sold antiques. I remember the musky smell of the shop. There was a particular daybed that I liked to play on. I also remember going for ice cream with my family. There was an ice cream shop on a boardwalk that was near a river. I would eat strawberry ice cream while sitting on a bench with my family. Then it came again—flash.

In my last vision, I was in the most beautiful place I have ever been. I don't have the words to describe it, but I will try. The blue sky above me was adorned with puffy white clouds, and the ground beneath my feet was spotless and shiny. Streams ran throughout, with bridges to cross them, and the people I saw were bright and glowing. To me, the closest way I could describe this beauty would be to compare it to a Japanese garden. However, it was dimensionless and bright. There was no suffering here, no stress or pain or mental anguish. Only peace.

I remember moving through this place in wonder. I could hardly believe what I saw and felt. It was so uplifting. There were people from all walks of life, creeds, and colors. Yes, from what I saw, Jews and Muslims were in harmony. They were walking about with intent like the white rabbit in *Alice in Wonderland*. You know the one, always in a hurry and famously saying, "Oh dear! Oh dear! I shall be late!" And while these people did not seem frustrated or rushed, it was clear they had very important things to do. The interesting thing about walking was that in reality I was still in my room on my bed. I had no legs to propel me. I guess our idea of mobility is to use what we have been using all our lives. I created a mental picture of moving.

As I was taking all of this in, I saw a group of people standing in a circle, heads bowed and eyes closed as they all held hands. They were praying. One woman broke from the group, turned around, and looked at me. She smiled.

She befriended me, and we walked together. She had an Eastern European accent, and I remember helping her find a passageway through a gate that seemed to run infinitely in both directions. But as I examined it, I found a small opening that allowed her to pass through. Then, everything went black.

I stood there alone in the darkness. On all sides of me was nothing but a black void, like a blanket of midnight covering myself and everything around me. As I looked ahead, my eyes straining against the utter darkness, I saw at last a bright light. My feet started moving toward it. For some reason, I knew I had to travel to that light, to stand in its lumens and let it envelop me. But getting there was difficult. My body felt weak and near failing, every step a desperate struggle against my own will. I suppose I made it, though, because soon—somehow and someway—I rose into the light. It was bright and peaceful, and when I stopped rising, I awoke from my coma.

When my faculties returned to the point where I could understand what was being said, my then fiancée came to visit me. I told her about my vision and this beautiful place I was in. I also told her about the people I met. She looked at me with sadness. She told me the woman I met was called Angelica. She was one of her best friends, and she was Polish.

Angelica was about 50 years old and had spent most of her life in a wheelchair. She was an author, who worked with orphans and was very spiritual. My fiancée spoke of her with great reverence and had apparently asked her and other members of her church to pray for me. She also told me that Angelica died the when I woke up from my coma. As I remembered the entryway through the gate I helped Angelica find in my vision, I considered that maybe she brought me back and I helped her enter the gates of heaven.

I will never forget the look on my fiancée's face. I don't know if it was shock, awe, or something else. In any event, she bent her head and I felt her tears drip onto my hand

CHAPTER FOUR

The hospital staff made it clear I would never be the same, whether it was with pitiful glances, grim expressions, or lines like "your mental acuity will not fully return" or "you'll never be able to walk without a cane." Of course, since I had awoken from the coma, that possible fate had haunted my thoughts, lingering ominously in the shadows of my mind. I wasn't willing, however, to simply accept this and fall into despair. I always survive chaos, after all.

The beginning was the hardest part. Summoning your body to move when you're that emaciated and weak is like driving with no gas or cashing a bad check. You just don't have what you need to pull it off. But I kept trying, and slowly, things got a little better. I got a big boost of confidence when my memory started to come back and I was able to sit up in bed. I would just sit there in silence, racking my brain for anything I could remember.

A large part of my time was spent meditating on my dreams and visions. Specifically, the one that led me out of my coma, the vision in which my fiancée's friend, Angelica, led me to the great light that brought me back, and in which I had also helped her find her way through a gate. And lastly, the fact that Angelica had recently passed—the very day I woke up. It was impossible for me to think this was all coincidence. So I wondered, more times than I could remember, if she had really helped me wake up—and if I had helped her move on from this earth.

A tall tale for someone else, perhaps, but after everything I had been through and seen, not so hard for me to consider.

Early on at the hospital, I tried to ignore the misfortune around me, choosing instead to dwell on improving my situation. It was like I slapped on mental blinders so I wouldn't get distracted, only focusing ahead on the most important goal I had ever set in my life—getting better. I wasn't daunted by this. It was more like me telling life, "Challenge accepted!" It gave me something to do. An activity, if you will. Something to strive for and a little experiment at the same time. And thus, I began my comeback.

Moving was a chore. I had wedges on either side to relieve the pressure off my bed sore, and I was stuck there and felt trapped. I had an air mattress that was slippery even with the bedding underneath me, and I used to slide down to the bottom of my bed and had to muster all my strength just to move up an inch. I had padded booties on my feet, and I remember my feet jamming into the footboard. My continuously trying to move myself all the way up to the top of the bed was a nonstop effort. I was in a constant state of discomfort—all day and all night. If I rolled to the right, I got vertigo and had to pause until it went away. My nights were composed of trying to sleep with the beeping of equipment, the hum of the air mattress, the alarms when my roommate tried to disconnect his support equipment, the IV and feeding bag changes, the medication, and my damn feet hitting the footboard. Let's not forget the pain and itching from my rash and bed sore.

I was on so much medication that it wiped me out. My resting pulse was 130 bpm, and there was medication for that, as well as pain meds which complicated everything. There were also meds to treat my drop in blood pressure when I sat up or stood. It was quite a dance Just sitting at the edge of the bed without falling over was a dance with gravity—and I wasn't leading. I finally got to the point where I could stand using a device that supported my weight. It was nice to stand but short-lived. Try to imagine what happens when you have been lying for so long and then you stand. Gravity takes hold. Your diaper fills. Your GI tract sinks. Your nose runs. What a mess.

I had developed a pressure wound on my butt the size of a grapefruit. You could actually see my hip joint through the hole. They would change my dressing every day, which meant rolling to my right, and that took me to dizzy city! They would scrub it and put on ointment and gauze. The entire procedure burned like hell. They would ask me, "On a one to ten scale, how much does it hurt?" It was always a ten, all day, every day! Once a week, the doctor would come in and remove the dead skin. He sprayed the wound with a freezing agent and tore the skin off with pliers. Industrial-strength agony! I wound up getting *Pseudomonas* and *Staphylococcus* infection in the wound. A nice green and tan color. Then it was more drugs, and with them, more side effects. At some point, I even got a UTI because of *Pseudomonas*. Curious how that infection moved from my back to my front. I needed a different set of antibiotics that came with, you guessed it, different side effects. Hospitals are dirty places. If you want to get an infec-tion, that's where you should go.

Another horrific issue was the logistics of moving my bowels. I was told, "Just go, you're on a pad, we'll clean it up." My God, another humiliation I had to endure. I remembered how proud I was when I used the potty when I was a kid, and to have that all change overnight and revert to before I was potty-trained was depressing. The problem was the texture, which was very messy and difficult to clean. My hands were too weak to use the call bell. So, I knocked. And waited. One hour. Two. Sometimes ten. Talk about trying times!

I would get washed daily, more rolling and dizziness. I was allergic to the washing agent, and I broke out in an itchy, burning, rash. Imagine lying on your back itching and burning with a bed sore. Forget "one to ten"—this was a twelve. That lasted three weeks, and all I could do was endure and carry on. Life goes on, after all. Maybe I just needed to appreciate the fact that I still existed. And then came the real question: did I want to exist in agony—or not at all? The one good thing that came out of it was that the aides used to tell me how wonderful my fiancée was, and that I was lucky to have her. That I already knew, but it was good to hear.

I started physical therapy on my arms and tried to regain some muscle tone. Slowly, my hands began to respond. I gained some weight in them, and they unfurled a little—although they still looked like bony hooks. At the same time, there were daily blood draws, catheter and IV changes and flushing, CAT scans, X-rays, and breathing and swallowing testing. I would get the mucous removed from my throat, and it made me cough and gag every time. I was hoping that this was not going to be my life. Up until that time, I'd had four intubations. So just swallowing saliva was a chore. My feeding tube was moved to my abdomen and would get snagged when I moved. Fun times!

My strength started to return, which made life easier—a bit! As I progressed, they changed my room three or four times. My last room had a window through which I could look outside. What a difference from the dark dank days of winter. It was certainly nice to see the glow of the sun and puffy white clouds. And birds, of course, coming and going as they performed their daily tasks. My cousins also started to visit, which was great for my morale, but you could see in their faces that they were in shock at the sight of me.

There was an aide who befriended me—a good guy who always asked me how I was and made conversation with me. When he asked me how I was doing, I could tell he really meant it, and it wasn't just a formality to break the silence while he attended to me. With some of the others, you could tell they were just going through the motions. Fake smiles and empty small talk. With this nurse, it was different, though. But one day he came in with a little black box tucked under his arm.

I knew whatever it was couldn't be good. I pondered morbidly about what kind of painful operation or procedure was in store for me. What manner of discomfort or unpleasantry I had to endure. But I was wrong. He smiled at me and opened the little case. Inside: grooming supplies. Then, he handed me a mirror.

I was aghast at what I saw—wondering if I had been transported to some strange world where mirrors showed you someone else rather than your own reflection. Because the man I saw looking back at me simply could not be myself. My beard was overgrown so much that my face was unrecognizable. My hair was overgrown as well, but because I had lost half of it, it was curiously long in some places and nearly bald in others. It had also turned much whiter. I took a deep breath and stared at the man in the mirror. Then, the aide got me cleaned up.

It was nice to get it all cut and look back in the mirror. For the first time in a long while, I felt human again. My goatee was back, and with it, a bit more of myself. My now-cut hair was still white and thinning, but oh well! After what I had been through, all good! I also remember that he brought in a radio one day, and what followed was a hospital room sing-along. We sang (or in my case tried to sing) Al Green, Marvin Gaye, and other classics. It was a soul revival! That was the first time I smiled in a very long time.

During my stay in the New Jersey hospital, my fiancée visited me less and less. Even though my house was about ten minutes from the hospital, she always seemed to have an excuse.

"Well, I just don't like your place," she went as far as to tell me one day. "I'd rather just commute from my place in New York."

I didn't know what to make of that. No, actually, I did. Something was amiss.

Our conversations became markedly more hostile. I felt like a toddler trying to parse adult language—helpless, slow, always behind. I could barely comprehend what she was saying or defend myself. I was just helpless and had to take a verbal beating. Even when I could process what she was saying, I couldn't seem to form any sort of argument or think quickly enough to respond. Seeing that I wasn't putting up a fight seemed to make her even more aggressive. She would yell in the hospital and humiliate me. With my mind not being back at a hundred percent, I knew I didn't have the energy to engage. My one sole purpose needed to be recovery and nothing else. So, I put my blinders back on, looked straight ahead at getting better, and let her ridiculousness fade to the periphery.

The time came to move me to a rehabilitation center. With my fiancée being absent, I had to make the decision. I was given a few choices, some of which I had been to when my dad needed nursing care. Most of them were outdated and smelled like urine. I reached out to a cousin who was a nurse, and she helped me make the decision. I wound up going to a place in Princeton, New Jersey, and I was transferred there at the end of April.

I traveled at night by ambulance, and as was my luck, we hit every bump and pothole possible along the way. My fiancée drove down separately and met us there. My relocation was a disaster. My room wasn't ready, and they didn't have my medication or simple things like oxygen. To her credit, my fiancée raised hell, and three hours later the issues were resolved. I was placed in a private room (at $1800 per day) because of the suspicion I may have had a *Clostridium difficile* infection, which I did not, thankfully. I guess the biggest thing I could never get used to was wearing a diaper. Changing me like a baby, cleaning me up, not getting all of it, and the itching and rashes that followed. All very humiliating.

They had to remove my tracheostomy. I remember them telling me to hold my breath, and with that, a big pull, lots of gagging, and it was finally out! What a relief, I could talk normally again, even if my throat was sore for weeks. My vision and hearing had returned, along with my mental acuity—as if to spite the nurses and doctors for everything they had said.

I was still on oxygen, and the pressure wound on my butt was so sore and painful that it throbbed with every movement.

Even though the rehab center was only 45 minutes from my house, my fiancée's visits were scarce. I had a room that faced southeast and had a big picture window. I would look out into the courtyard, and wouldn't you know it, I made friends. Not nurses or patients or other humans at all. No, my new friends were of a different variety.

There was a garden and a gazebo, and about two days into my stay, I started seeing cardinals. There was a male and a female, and they visited every day. They would sit on the branches and let out an unmistakable chirp. My mom used to say that cardinals are your past relatives visiting you, which was a nice thought to consider. Whether past relatives or not, they made me smile and gave me peace when I saw them. My bed, about 12 feet from the door, was positioned parallel to the window, so it was easy to look out. My bathroom was next to the door. That 12 feet might as well have been 10 miles, for I could not walk it. So close yet so far!

As a result of my ordeal, I was, and still am, very claustrophobic. I had to sleep (what little I got) with a light on and the door open. Every day I would battle with the nurse and aides to keep the door open and the light on. Never a dull moment. Too bad the cardinals were not out at night. They would've brought me peace. Needless to say, the other patients always complained, but with the amount I paid daily, I couldn't care less!

The rehab center, much like the hospitals, was not the cleanest place. It was understaffed, lacking inventory (lab gowns, gloves, etc.), and a good portion of the staff was undertrained. It was not uncommon to have one aide for 80 people over the weekend. That meant having to sit in your feces for twelve hours, no refills on water, and sparse bathing and brushing your teeth. To circumvent the water situation, I had a case of water brought in. However, I was too weak to open the bottles. Like some bedridden mob boss, I had to bribe the night aide with chocolate to open them and leave them on the night table. Changings were a chore, and the aides hated them even more than I did. One time, a new aide came in all pissed off having to change my diaper. She ripped it off and threw it over the bed, and it hit the wall with a *splat!* My shit stayed on the wall like a Jackson Pollock tribute to institutional neglect—for three damn days .

By this time, I was cognizant enough to scrutinize my medications. I checked the prescriptions I was given and their dosages, and I'm glad I did. I was given the wrong script—and the wrong amount—and I had overdosed! I squawked about it and was told that was all they had. Apparently, there was no pharmacy on site, and it had to be ordered. I still couldn't swallow so they administered the medication through my feeding tube. They would connect a syringe, add my crushed-up medications dissolved in water, and push it all in. Imagine being warm and then getting 100 cc of cold water injected into your stomach. The flush was even worse. Some nurses had better aim than others, meaning a cold bath was often incoming. Brr!! I was still getting blood thinners injected too, and my abdomen stayed purple for two months after my discharge.

They also added a wound vac. As the name implies, it assisted in healing by applying suction to remove fluids and promote tissue growth. Every two days, the nurses would remove the bandage and add a new one. It was made of plastic and would also seal the wound. The hard part was adding a sponge into the wound before sealing it. Like I said, on a scale of one to ten my butt was a twelve. I realized this would help me heal, but sleeping? No way. Not even a chance. It also meant no showers until I was healed! Baby wipes became my friend. I had the air mattress hum, the pump buzz, the oxygen scrubber clanging away, and the usual vitals, IV, and feeding changes. Let's not forget the facility was also long-term care and there was a lot of screaming at night! And I mean real screaming, as if the patients I was hearing were being tormented by medieval torture devices.

I was taken off the liquid diet and was actually able to eat on my own. However, everything was thickened or ground up. One step forward and two steps back! I was fed eggs every morning for ninety days. Water and coffee thickened, food ground! I think the very concept of thickened water is lost to most. Thankfully, most of you will never have occasion to experience it. Instead of drinking a refreshing liquid, you have to swallow down a viscous glop. Think of trying to drink down an unruly blob of thick gel, like a Jello shot without the shot. Exactly. It was as terrible as it sounds.

And the food was another story. Ever have cold chicken, broccoli, and potatoes ground up? Disgusting! I had more food on me than I had eaten. I had to swallow by turning my head to the left and down, and I had difficulty holding utensils and cups. Remember, my fingers were still curled and weak, and many times, I failed at the simple task of grabbing a fork. Seeing myself struggle with meals made me have a vision of my aunt when she ate. She had crooked fingers, so we cut her food, and she used to pick up her cup by placing her index finger in the cup and the rest of her fingers outside of it. Not a far cry from the way I was eating now. The thought that this would be my life forever crept further into my consciousness, no longer sneaking quietly, but boldly announcing its presence. How long could I ignore this possibility and stay positive?

I remember testing to see if I could eat solid food, and it took a whole week. Why? Because the tester had two jobs, and I was her second. It sucked. At $1800 per day, and I was still basically ignored. I finally passed the test, and by this time, I had lost about 35% of my body weight (about 80 pounds). Now I could eat normally, but again, being able to use a knife was a chore in itself. My fiancée visited occasionally, and once she brought me a hamburger, fries, and a coke from Five Guys. That was the first meal that wasn't hospital food that I'd had. But because I had lost so much weight and my stomach shrank, I only had a couple of bites, and I was done. I never thought I would say fast food was heavenly, but it was!

Then I began physical and occupational therapy. The therapists were great, and therapy gave me a mission and a focus. I remember my first evaluation. I couldn't sit up or stand, which was concerning to all. One physical therapist actually told me if I didn't show improvement, Medicare wouldn't pay for it, and I would have to leave. Can you imagine? I hadn't even been there for one week and I had to worry about Medicare!

I remember the first time I sat up. It was everything! When you're weak, you have very little control. I was like a boat taking on water—fine for a couple of minutes, then listing to the side. It happened every time. The therapists would try to catch me before I hit my head. Every so often, they would miss and I would fall over and hit my head with a thud. It was frustrating as hell. Before I went into the hospital,

I could bang out 100 sit-ups without a sweat. Oh well. That was then, and this is now. I took what I could get, and every day there were cardinals!

We trained from my bed for about one month. I would lie and use elastics, which led to weights. As my muscles got stronger, my exercise became sitting up and balancing. Then, there was exercising while sitting up. There is a saying: "For every day in bed you need three days to get back to where you were originally." Needless to say, I had a long way to go. We gradually went to using the wheelchair, and there was a specific process to get into it. I imagined what it would be like to be a tightrope acrobat, where a slip and fall was just one movement away. Because that was my biggest concern—falling. I was always worried about falling. But I got through it, and my confidence started to build.

We focused on strength and the ability to perform household tasks. This unfortunately showed me how we take everything for granted. Our balance, stamina, hand-eye coordination, strength, and memory all work together to make possible nearly everything we do, and I was learning the hard way what it was like to be without these privileges. It was like everything I had developed from the time I was a baby disappeared, and I was an infant again. I started to use the wheelchair more and more. I would roll into the bathroom by myself (and my wound vac) and try to perform basic functions, all the while looking at my appalling self in the mirror. I don't know how I got through it, and it definitely tested my soul. I remember the first time I was able to use the toilet. I felt like I did when I was a toddler using the potty for the first time, except this time I received no cheers, hugs, kisses, or "attaboys". But it was certainly nice to feel independent and human again!

At the same time, I began to get steadily stronger. I managed to stand for ten seconds, then twenty, and from there I was able to get into a wheelchair. I felt like I did when I got my driver's license. Freedom! I received a set of rosary beads from my cousin, and I started carrying them and, for the first time in years, praying the Rosary every night. I figured I could use all the help I could get. From there came walking. Two steps with a walker, then four. Then twelve feet to the door. Each time, the physical therapist would put me in the wheelchair and wheel me back. Invigorating! I remember the exhaustion and clinging to my oxygen.

One day, I had a breakthrough. I walked to the door and back without my oxygen or wheelchair. That's right, twenty-four feet! We started increasing the distance. Twenty feet and back with a wheelchair. Then twenty feet without it. This went on for a month. I ended up walking one hundred and twenty feet, twice a day. Unstoppable! I kept thinking about the hospital staff talking about me being bedridden and institutionalized. I thought about Rodney Dangerfield's line in *Back to School*, "I ain't taking shit from anyone, I am going to pass this test!"

Next came the gym and coordination and strength training. I would wheel myself down to the gym with rosary in hand. Yes, I was truly mobile! I did weight training and coordination drills. Initially, there was an exercise in which I had to hold myself up and put some disks on sticks, and I never thought anything could be so fatiguing. I got through it, though. Squats were quite a task, but if I wanted to get out of bed myself, it needed to be done. Passed that too. Then, the dreaded stairs. On my first attempt, I failed, fell, and split open my elbow. A bloody mess. Wounds and blood thinners are not good soul mates. With assistance, I completed my second attempt to climb the stairs. It was only four steps, and I got it done. It was all success after that. I still wasn't able to climb a full flight. That would have to come later.

We also switched over to a walker with wheels and continued my distance walking. Finally, the therapists took me outside to practice walking on uneven sidewalks, stepping up and down curbs, and getting in and out of a car. I hadn't been outside since December of 2021. It was as close to perfect as it could get. I must admit that the mental part was harder than the physical. Always worrying about not being able to do it, or even worse, falling. Think about it like walking on black ice. You know you are going to slip; it is only a matter of when.

There was a weekly weighing, and I would hold my breath each time. They would put me in a harness and connect me to a lift where I would just hang and swing in the wind. It reminded me of *Caddyshack* where Rodney Dangerfield had the same experience and said, "Hey, while I'm up here, change my oil!" That was probably the first time I was looking forward to gaining weight. My total gains were 15 pounds!

One night, I had a scare that came closer than the screams outside my room. I drifted awake with a strange feeling of self-consciousness. You know the feeling of someone standing behind you or the sense that everyone's looking at you? That's the one. My eyelids fluttered open slowly, then sprung wide. Two guys in wheelchairs were staring in my face!

Then, they wheeled off casually, as if nothing had happened, and I was left to wonder just what in the world was going on. *Now it's getting weird*, I thought. *I have to get the hell out of here!*

I had been there for about two weeks when they decided it was time to remove my catheter. When a female nurse says you will feel a slight sensation, time to worry. Well, it felt like someone had grabbed my penis with pliers. Slight sensation, my butt! It was nice to be able to pee on my own, but that came with its own issues. The peeing itself wasn't the problem—it was the aiming. And about four days after they took out my catheter, I got a urinary tract infection. I have heard of infection when inserting, but not on removal.

One day, a conversation with the attending physician made me worry. She wanted to proceed with what she deemed as standard antibiotic therapy for my UTI. The issue was that I worked on the discovery of antimicrobial antibiotics for three decades and was an expert in the field. We discussed the type of bacterial infection I had and its resistance to certain antibiotics. We also discussed treatment, and I implored her not to do what they do in Japan—underdose with a short duration. But she didn't listen and went by the approved therapy outlined in her therapy card. So, my UTI wasn't cured and became chronic. I struggled through ninety days of therapy with various IV and oral antibiotics.

Nothing is more frustrating than knowing how to prevent something bad from happening to you, but because those in charge of your care don't have the same knowledge, it happens anyway. After the doctor failed to heed my advice, I had to sit back and watch as they made everything worse. And worse it truly became. Not only did they fail to cure my infection with antibiotic therapy, but they also sent me home after ninety days still infected.

My fiancée assumed being my primary care person early on and, to her credit, she came every day while I was in New

York City. However, visits were few and far between as I became cognizant of my care and surroundings. When I went to rehab, she would visit, and her hostility escalated. She searched my entire house and would complain about my bills, money, what I did in my free time, my businesses, and anything else she could. She would bring me my mail and start an argument with me over it.

One day, she came to visit with my suitcase. In it she had my mail, which she started pulling out. I had about twelve letters from lawyers threatening lawsuits. Apparently, if you don't pay your creditors in three months, they freeze your credit, and after four months it goes to collections. Before I went into the hospital, my credit score was 805 and my average credit account was 25 years old. Now this! On top of it all, my fiancée pulled out an old will that was about forty years old. I had gone through a difficult split and just couldn't deal with changing my will and forgot about it. She got pissed because her name wasn't on it. A red flag? Please. She was a matador—waving a red cape and provoking drama at every turn.

She went on to say that she did all this for me and my ex would get everything. Was she serious? Was she actually serious? After all, she never changed her own will, and now I'm obligated to change mine—or else I had to deal with her anger? My lawyer told me the new will should not be signed until we wed because she had no right to anything. One humorous thing, if there is any humor in it at all, is she had also brought a metal box with a big padlock on it.

"What's this?" she snarled.

I found the entitlement to demand what one of *my* belongings was, the anger in her voice as spittle sprayed, and the aggression shown by the intense look in her wide eyes simply mind-blowing. But I only smirked. "That's my ammo box," I told her. "And you're transporting it without a license."

That shut her up for a while, but not long enough. So, there I was worrying about getting better, and then all of that added craziness too! I thought I was going to explode. I knew we were falling apart when I didn't see her during the holidays. I got a call telling me she was going on vacation with her son for the Fourth of July, and I knew I was going to be alone. I guess better then than now!

As if I didn't have enough stuff going on, the air conditioner in my room broke. After four attempts, the brainiacs concluded that it couldn't be fixed. At this point, it was easy to think that the universe was conspiring against me in some awful way. Had to be. They brought in a portable unit and installed it in an open window. It was either 90 degrees or 64 degrees—no in between. In addition, there was lots of pollen, as if breathing wasn't difficult enough. I guess no rest for the weary!

About one month before I was discharged, I started to see more cardinals! I figured they were the young from the ones I initially began to see daily. There was a male and a female. The male was black with a dark red breast. The female was also dark with black wings and a deep red breast that faded to black. I had never seen that before. At first, I thought they were crows. Then their distinctive chirp gave it away and, in addition, they had those pointy heads unique to cardinals. The cardinal family were daily guests, and I welcomed them very much.

My progress continued each day for the rest of my stay. My cousins and friends started to come around, and I was getting daily calls. After everything I had been through, it was an exciting time. I remember being able to wash in front of the sink, shave, and brush my teeth. I was even able to use the toilet. You can't imagine being free from diapers. The stigma of wearing those and having to depend on someone to change you was the worst. Humiliating and depressing is all I can say. I finally was able to wear a T-shirt and gym shorts. I didn't feel like a patient any more, just a boarder who was moving on. It was the best by far. One day, my neighbor and her daughter stopped by to see me with my fiancée. I was told that my neighbor's daughter, Abby, would stay with me when I was released to take care of me. She was attending nursing school at the time. It had been arranged by my fiancée, and I guess it was her way of further backing out.

And so it was that we made plans for my discharge. I worked diligently to show progress and to pass all the necessary testing. I also was allowed 90 days of care by Medicare standards. I was told that if I stayed home for 60 days, I could come back for another 90 days. Yeah right! That place was never seeing me again if I could help it. I ordered a rolling walker and some occupational gear to help at home. I got a long shoehorn, a grabber to pick stuff up, and a sock assist to help me put on my socks. I had to demonstrate I could use them before leaving. They also gave me a home version of my wound vac, for I would need it until I healed (6 more months). Then we planned the day of my discharge, July 27, 2022. Almost seven months to the day I started this "journey". I had to order a hospital bed for home, along with an air mattress, a wheelchair, a bench for showering, and a commode extension. I had one more walking test and an evaluation. I would have to wear a brace on my left leg and use a walker. The rest would be up to me and home physical and occupational therapy.

One last medical procedure was required. I had to have the feeding tube removed from my abdomen. So, think about it, I walked around with this capped rubber tube hanging from the middle of my chest—right below my ribs—for 90 days. It passed through my abdomen and into my stomach, and it had an inflatable balloon on the other side to hold it in place. The procedure was to deflate the balloon and pull it out. Like everything else, it did not go smoothly. The doctor had difficulty removing it, and she actually had to climb up on the bed, hold me down with one hand, and yank as hard as she could. Finally, I heard a pop, and out it came. At long last, I was disconnected from the hospital, at least for now. After the wound healed, I discovered that I had become the proud owner of two belly buttons.

The day before my discharge, all four cardinals came to see me. I remember the chirps as they landed one at a time. I guess it was their way of saying goodbye and good luck. It had been a long and difficult road, and I thanked God I got through it. I had made friends and lost friends. Such is life! On Wednesday the 27th of July, I was released from the center. I used the their wheelchair to leave and took the rest of my belongings.

To my surprise, my fiancée gave me a ride home. Oddly enough, it was nice to see her, and the trip home was cordial. My lease had run out on the car she was using, so she had bought a new car. It was an SUV, which made it easy to get into. We small-talked for the entire ride. I remember my butt hurting from all the bumps on the way home. When we turned onto my street, nothing had ever looked better. I had bought a family home, and there it was in the middle of the block. A big white monolith attesting to my life. What a sweet sight!

I relished the feeling and took it all in, but soon I had work to do. Then came the anguish of going up a six-stepped walkway from the street followed by a six-step front porch. Talk about anxiety! We figured out a way to use the walker for the first step, then I would sit in a chair on the second step until the walker came up, and repeat. Then came the steps into the house. Same thing, chair on the top step, then I would climb and pull myself up the six stairs. Then sit. I was completely out of breath and dizzy, but I finally made it into the house.

It is a multi-level home with the master bedroom on the second floor, and my fiancée, Abby, and her cousin had rearranged the first floor by turning my living room into my bedroom and temporarily putting a lot of furniture in the sunroom. We also had to do some modifications to the bathroom—door removal, commode extension, and so on. Still, it was home sweet home. I found the bed and collapsed in it. I couldn't believe I was home. I remember Abby made me a welcome home poster that I still have on the wall in my exercise room. It's a constant reminder of where I was and where I am now, and makes me think of these words from my favorite poem: "I'll rise and fight again."

CHAPTER FIVE

I had naively thought that coming home would be the end of my struggles. The final milestone and conclusion to my hurdles. A respite from the ongoing storm. And while the clouds did part briefly, allowing the sun to shine down upon me for a moment or two, they soon darkened and thickened back to an overcast sky. I was free from the hospital and rehab center, you see, but not from my suffering. And among everything that had happened, perhaps the most disappointing of all was that even though I was finally home, there were no cardinals outside my window to visit me.

But I couldn't give up. I have always believed that you can get mired in self-pity and let it consume you, or just keep going. I survived a coma, a stroke, a tracheotomy, blood clots, bed sores, and more than one brush with death. I got out of rehab before they killed me. And now I was home with the same lingering issues I had in both the hospital and in rehab. I would make it through this, too, or die in the attempt.

It took me a while to settle into my new living arrangement. Inhabiting the living room was difficult. The air mattress they gave me had a hole in it and collapsed, and I had to sleep on metal bars for three days until they replaced it.

Imagine having an open wound and lying on metal bars. Three nights of that, and I started to understand medieval torture. Learning how to navigate my house with a wheelchair took time. The house was not set up for a wheelchair, and now I know why my neighbors moved out once they required one. Everything was different. Just simple things like washing up in the bathroom or getting something to drink was an obstacle. I would get fatigued all the time.

When I was released, my flexibility was completely gone. I couldn't even cross my legs to put on my socks. I had to use a plastic device that was about 12 inches long and curved like a PVC pipe split down the middle. It had a rope tied to either side, and I would have to thread my sock onto it and slip it up and over my foot. As I pulled the rope, the sock would slide up my leg. To pick things up, I had this hook with a pistol grip. I was stiff as a board. Have you ever tried to grab tiny pills with a hook? I used to stick tape to it to pick them up. Same thing with the shoehorn. It was 30 inches long and worked well. I figure I had about 10 seconds before my breath ran out, and I got cramps between my ribs when tying my shoe.

I used to divide my days into routines, breaking everything down into the least number of steps or tasks so I could be economical with my activities. I also ran scenarios in my head as to what to do if something happened. For example, you cannot imagine the production it took just to retrieve a pillow I dropped behind the bed—without falling, mind you. But, through it all, I started settling in! And I also got a special visitor. I would leave my front door open to get sunlight and look out from my bed and, wouldn't you know it, I saw a familiar sight. Yep, a cardinal landed on the railing of my front porch. I had never seen that in all the time I lived there—there were cardinals, but they were always flying or in the trees. It gave me peace, and I knew I was on the right path!

I had developed a daily routine. I would get up and wheel into the bathroom, do the needful, and even wash my hair. For my reward, I would sit in the wheelchair and catch my breath. Next, I would wheel into the kitchen and make breakfast. While the coffeemaker was dripping, I would pour a bowl of cereal. Rice Krispies! I never thought that *snap*, *crackle*, and *pop* could sound so good. The things you take for granted! At that point, I had been home for two weeks, and I needed to work. So, I called the company I used to work for, and I reacquired my old position as consultant. I consulted on bio-technology, automation and robotics, and information technology. I think they were as glad to have me back as I was to return. It was ideal in that I was familiar with the work and could do it from home.

At the same time, I started to feel really bad. It felt like the flu, and it just kept getting worse. Then it was back to the hospital—my old toxic lover had just come back. I went into the emergency room with aches and chest pains, and I was in the ER for 24 hours before they made a decision. There is a test they did for heart events called a troponin test that measures the troponin in your blood. Troponin is a protein that's released into your bloodstream during a heart attack. It requires three separate blood draws over the course of nine hours.

They also ran blood and urine tests, an EKG, and took X-rays. The urine test was for microbial growth, which took five days. Thus, I had to wait until the next week before all my results came back. They indicated I needed further testing. I had to get a cardiac catheterization which was scheduled on a

Tuesday. At the same time, my bloodwork showed I had stage three kidney disease. And just like that, a new dance began!

I was given medication to raise my kidney function because the dye they use in catheterization can cause kidney damage. The medicine was horrible. It had a strong sulfuric smell, and the taste was even worse. I figured out a way to make the medication more palatable by adding it to ginger ale. My procedure was scheduled for noon, and I remember praying that it would turn out well, and of course, I had my rosary for protection. I must have dozed off during the wait because I was stirred awake by a gentle voice. I opened my eyes, and a priest stood over me. I remember him praying and anointing me with oil. I took it as God's way of saying that I would get through this.

We went to the catheterization lab for testing, and I remember the coldness of the room and all the masked faces. This time, the procedure went through my right wrist. I remember them calling out the equipment they were using, the beeping of the monitors, and the anesthetist telling me to be calm. I am not easy to sedate. It frustrates the doctors every time. We ended up doing the procedure while I was awake, and yes, it was as horrible as it sounds. To my chagrin, the anesthesia wore off and I felt everything going in and out of my wrist. What a day!

That night, my cardiologist told me that nothing had changed. So, what was the problem, you ask? Well, my infection came back. Same bacterium, same drug resistance as in rehab. They sent me home with antibiotics that didn't work, and I got worse and worse until they found an appropriate therapy. I eventually felt better and went on with my life, and I hoped that would be the end of it.

I was also still settling in at home and running the house. Paying bills, getting groceries, scheduling deliveries, and suchlike. I don't know how I did it, but it got done. I also had to put up with all the calls about delinquencies. I had most of my creditors for 25 years. I had American Express for over 50 years, but despite this, they were the absolute worst to deal with. First of all, I was speaking to representatives who were 25 years old and seemed to be clueless about the gravity and importance of a long-term client relationship. It didn't matter that I was hospitalized or was never late before, only that I was late now and needed to pay. They only cared about when I could make a payment. I got three or four calls a day.

I had entered into forbearance to cover my mortgage payment, and the bank extended me for one year. Physical money was an issue. If I needed cash, I had to get a transport service (at $150 per trip) to take me and bring me back, and I also had to find a service that would pick me up in a wheelchair. Doctor visits were the same. I started with four doctors, which grew to fourteen by the end of the year. For the year, it cost me about $6,000 in transportation (rides, deliveries, etc.).

I distinctly remember visiting my doctors. Some were new, and others I had known for over 30 years. I was so thin and frail and could see that on their faces—like I was looking in a mirror every time I made eye contact with one of them. I knew I was in bad shape by the shock reflected in their eyes just by looking at me. One doctor, who has taken care of my dad and me for over 40 years said, "Jesus, Mike, you look like you have cancer." Yeah, it was that bad, for I was only a fraction of my usual 240 pounds. But what could I do? That was the first time a cardiologist told me to eat what I wanted and that I needed to gain weight.

I also had the sudden realization that I was going to have to do something that I really didn't want to do—file for bankruptcy! I always believed that was not the way to go. That was for people who mismanaged their finances and were looking for a way out. Well, there I was being sued personally and professionally by my creditors. I had exhausted my funds, lost my job for 8 months, and had crazy medical bills. I was pushed into a corner with no recourse but to file. I asked my business lawyer for advice, and yes, he recommended the dreaded "B".

It took me a month to find a local bankruptcy lawyer. Lawyers are a motley bunch, and they range in a spectrum from truly wanting to help others to truly wanting to help themselves. You know when they ask how much you owe and want a retainer before advising you that it is the latter. Luckily, I found myself the former. Believe me, filing for bankruptcy is not easy. It took six months of paperwork to file and another three months to be granted a Chapter 13. I needed five years of tax statements, current liabilities versus income, bank statements, projections on income, insurance and investment plans, property estimates, and on and on.

On top of all that, I had to give updates until it was granted. I still have a trustee who is the equivalent of a parole officer. He monitors everything. I had to go through my lawyer to speak to him. Both had fees, and we would modify my monthly payment depending on my savings. I still have to pay my back taxes. I can't go on trips, can't get any credit, and if I need a car, I have to go through him. I certainly can't move. If I sell my house before the bankruptcy is discharged, my creditors can come after the proceeds. One step forward and two steps back!

What was next on the menu was grueling—six months of physical and occupational therapy, six days a week. I would also require six months of nursing care to clean and seal my pressure wound, and speaking of six months, it took six months to be able to shower, cook, and clean by myself. A visiting nurse would come in three times a week to get a status update and to change my dressing—which was always an ordeal. There was ordering supplies, the physical changing (again, a twelve on a one to ten scale of pain), and making sure there were no vacuum leaks. Due to all the supplies and boxes everywhere, my home looked like a warehouse.

I remember the glue for my bandages used to stick to my gym shorts. The first couple of times, when disrobing, I would accidentally pull the bandage and break the seal. That led to quite an effort to get a visiting nurse to come back and fix it. Again, I had to develop a disrobing process. I had to slip my crippled fingers in the back and pull the glue free. I could only stand for a short period of time, so everything had to be completed quickly to avoid pulling the bandage off. My hand looked like a garden rake. Imagine putting a rake down your pants and trying to separate a bandage from your shorts. Fun times!

I also had two nurses come twice a week each for physical and occupational therapy. In the beginning, it was tough going. My blood pressure dropped each time I stood, so all my exercises were either in bed or sitting down. Gradually, I started to get my strength back. With all the exercise, my blood pressure stabilized, and I could stand without fainting. After five months, I didn't need occupational therapy anymore, and I was released. One down and one to go. In October, my physical therapist got me up and using a walker.

We had a set path I would use: walk around the house, around the living room, up and down the hall, into the dining room, and back.

The laps increased each day, and I ditched the walker for a cane, which felt like swapping a prison guard for a dance partner. We worked on leg strengthening and climbing the dreaded stairs. Up one step and down, up two steps and down. By December, I could climb the thirteen steps up to the second floor. That was the first time I was able to do that. It took ten months to confidently climb a flight of stairs. There was still finetuning I needed to do, like learning to carry things while I ascended, but wow, I was almost there!

That December was mild by New Jersey's standards, and my therapist took me out for a walk. It was both elating and terrifying. Walking in the safety of my home was not the same as uneven steps and streets. The first time I went outside in a vertical position gave me a rush. We mastered the steps on the staircase down the porch, and then the stairs on the sidewalk. When I got to the street, the first thing I did was turn around and look at the house. It filled me with happiness and pride to behold my home, especially considering the trials I had endured and overcome to make it back there.

We then started walking up and down the street, measuring my progress by the number of telephone poles I passed. I was excited to check my weekly progress. At the same time, there was always the fear of passing the point of no return. In other words, I feared walking too far and not being able to walk back. But I did—I got through it. I could walk with a cane, and I felt truly free! In retrospect, I miss my therapists. I guess friendships are formed through trial by fire. You work toward a common goal, share experiences, and become friends. I can't thank them enough. With my new freedom, I didn't need a wheelchair service anymore. I could fit into an Uber XL, and I had gained freedom and the savings of paying $35 versus $150 per trip!

Home wasn't the quiet I was used to. I basically had a roommate, because Abby was living on the second floor. She was very welcoming and did the best she could. She also started going back to nursing school and had to split her time. Like many young people, she had a lot going on, and her schedule often included staying up late and making noise. The heavy toilet seat in the second-floor bathroom thudded sharply every night at two a.m., jolting me awake. But besides such minor inconveniences, she was great. She would make me lunch and dinner and we would eat together—me using a tray on my bed and Abby at the table. We became friends, which helped me get through such a trying time. We had our difficulties, as all roommates do, which brings me to the topic of a long, furry animal with a spine like a slinky snake. I'm talking about a ferret, of course, and she had two of them! I didn't know about them until they came down one day to visit. Little biting, squeaking things, but it was better than two old dudes in wheelchairs screaming and staring in my face.

I began to help her study. She would do her reading and come down and ask questions about the material. We would go through her notebook, and she would teach me about what she was learning. I love being a mentor! The amount of purpose I felt helping a young person on their journey was unparalleled, and I relished our little study sessions. All in all, I'm glad Abby came to help out, even though there was trouble looming right around the corner. Safe to say, things really started to stink.

One day, there was an awful smell coming from the basement. When I looked, I saw five inches of raw sewage on the floor. I had to call my insurance and a service to clean it up. You see, Abby had used baby wipes and flushed them. The damages were $2,500 for the plumber and $16,000 to clean it all up! I had to strip everything out of the basement. My life, oh boy! After a big fight with my fiancée, Abby and her mom thought it was best for her to move out. I was sad to see her go. We still keep in touch, and she is an RN at a New York City hospital now. Good for her!

While all this was happening, I started on a routine of doctor visits. When you get old, you don't have a doctor, you have a collection of "ologists". Cardiologists, gastroenterologists—specialists for every imaginable condition. I started the rounds, which led to other "ologists". When I was done, I had 14 of them. There were medication changes and adjustments, testing, and theories on my symptoms. No one knew about the long-term effect of COVID, but they attributed my new symptoms to it anyhow. They checked my circulation, my heart, my GI system, my lungs, and so on. I went to a neurosurgeon, a neurologist, and a neuropsychiatrist. The neurosurgeon didn't find anything new, but the nerve tests from my neurologist indicated severe nerve damage from my knees down. As for my psychiatric evaluation—it was interesting. Somehow, I was able to integrate and remember information more easily. But that doesn't mean I don't still go into rooms and wonder why I am there!

I had trouble swallowing. Apparently, the multiple intubations and stroke had caused scar tissue to form in my esophagus and compromised swallowing. So, I had to have my esophagus stretched. Into the hospital again. I spoke with a doctor and asked if I had anything to worry about. That was a mistake. He said, "Yes, your esophagus could rupture. By the way, do we have your blood type?" I should not have asked. Sometimes, little things can be so defeating!

An interesting phenomenon was that I went into the hospital with dyslexia, and when I came out, it was gone. The theory is that the reason I was in a coma for so long was because I was rewiring my brain function. How about that? I do feel different, to be honest. I can recall more easily and have better short-term memory. I also have a lot more confidence and am much calmer. Speaking of being calm, I am the product of Italian parents from Newark, New Jersey, and I have never had any patience for nonsense. For example, I worked for a colleague (ex-colleague now) who didn't pay me for three months. When confronted, he refused. He wouldn't answer the phone or reply to my emails. What did I do? Well, I figured I would send him a more convincing message, so I pulled his mailbox out of the ground and put it on the porch of the nearest funeral home. Needless to say, he paid in two days.

All my doctors did agree on one thing, namely that I am alive because of all the muscle mass I had. My body lived off it while I was in my coma. It felt good to think that I had built up my body to be strong enough to endure, and yet it was still bittersweet, after going through everything I had.

I tried to celebrate the holidays, which I hoped would bring a feeling of normalcy into my life. My birthday is in October, and to my surprise, my now ex-fiancée came over with my best friend and his wife. It was so great to host them at my house. I felt things were looking up, and better times were on the way. Next was Halloween—my favorite holiday. I ordered candy from Amazon, the large-size Kit-Kat bars, and

I sat on my walker (it had a seat) with the front door open. I must have had 100 kids clamoring for treats. It was the best!

I was alone on Thanksgiving and ordered takeout. What else but Chinese food with memories of *A Christmas Story* in my head? It was the movie I watched while eating, too! Finally, Christmas came, and I ordered flowers for my relatives, friends, and my ex-fiancée and wrote out Christmas cards. I usually decorate, but I couldn't manage it. I ordered a live tree and a string of lights from Home Depot. It looked like a Charlie Brown Christmas tree, but I didn't care. I have special Christmas ornaments of my mom, my dad, and my dog, and that was enough adornment to make it perfect. After everything I had been through, life was good!

Next up was healing the pressure wound on my behind. I had to visit the local hospital for a wound specialist to assess my progress. He had the same opinion as my visiting nurses because the wound was still open, and he gave it a stage four rating. However, it was healing slowly and starting to close from the inside. There was a big concern about how the wound would heal. It had to heal from the inside. If it didn't, I would need surgery to open it up, and I would have to go through the entire process again. Something else to add to my prayer list!

I went to the wound specialist every month for 7 months, and my ass was out for all to see. I figure most of New York and New Jersey have seen my ass. Great! I'm sure I traumatized a lot of people. My bare ass aside, every month, my wound became a little better. And, slowly, it finally healed.

My doctor was an older Italian guy who was delighted at my respect and my attempt at speaking Italian. One day in January, he leaned over and said, "Finito." I couldn't believe it. He completely disconnected me from my wound vac (or Bob, as I lovingly called it). No more visits, and I could finally shower. He did caution me to be careful because it was still healing inside and warned me not to fall on it. I got home that day and ripped my clothes off. Straight into the shower. I had to maneuver myself onto the shower bench, but who cares? I must have sat for an hour! It was so nice! I was starting to feel human again. The best part of all was that I got to move upstairs and reclaim a bit of my old life!

I couldn't wait to return the bed and wheelchair. I couldn't get rid of them fast enough. I moved upstairs, and everything had this musky smell. I had to sleep downstairs in the spare bedroom until I could clean it up. I had to replace my queen-sized bed in the master, as well as my full-sized bed in the front bedroom due to the smell and biting damage. I needed new area rugs, the entire upstairs repainted, and the molding replaced. The total cost was $6,500. Damn ferrets!

I rearranged all the furniture, and my house became a home again. I love plants, and I have many. Unfortunately, they had not been watered for seven months. They all came back, though, as if they were waiting for me. I have a giant jade plant that I have had since 1980. I'd like to believe it was glad to see me.

While all of this was going on, my relationship with my fiancée fell apart. She told me she couldn't do it anymore, and we were done.

CHAPTER SIX

I can't blame my fiancée for leaving, although I would've done it differently. The reasons on her part were suspect. I guess when you take things out of context, they can blow up really quickly, and arguments start to feel never-ending. There is a saying, "Show me a person, and I'll find something wrong with them," and that's what it felt like with her. She told me she had wasted three years of her life with me. I could hardly believe she used the word "wasted". If you really love a person, can time spent with them ever be a waste? All of this happened by the end of September, and I was gutted. I always believed that if you truly love someone, you will find a reason to stay! Perhaps I am naïve or overly romantic, but that is what I believe. Apparently, love isn't enough. Who knew? During the winter of 2022/2023, I started walking outside (I still do, weather permitting). I would walk the same road that my physical therapist and I took. I had the confidence to do that much. It was wonderful to be outside walking on my own. Just me and my cane. I saw old neighbors coming and going, and they would all ask how I was coming along. I also met my new neighbors. If anyone ever says you don't need neighbors, they are so totally wrong. The sense of community, camaraderie, and support they provide is unparalleled. As for the neighborhood itself, it had certainly changed. A few houses were bought at a bankruptcy sale, and I felt sorry for those who had lost their homes. I know all too well what they went through.

My house is my childhood home I purchased when my mom passed. My dad was going to lose it because he couldn't cope financially without her pension and social security. When I bought it, there was an understanding that my dad and aunt could stay as long as they wanted. I suppose that I am one of the oldest neighbors, and my family was the original owner. In total, I have lived there for 69 years. I have been neighbors with some for over 50 years. Time flies!

My neighborhood is very quiet and peaceful. Every time I go out, I think about when I was a kid. We used to skateboard, bike, and play baseball and football, and walking around and remembering those memories is like strolling back in time. Of course, I have to mention the neighborhood birds, the best of which are the cardinals. Like my own family, there are established bird families that have been in the neighborhood for years. The cardinals make themselves known with flashes of red accompanied by their distinguishing chirps. Whenever I see or hear them, it is like my relatives are with me!

When I walked, I would set milestones. I would push it a little farther each time, all the while being cognizant of my point of no return. First, it was up the hill to the end of the road and back. Next, halfway around the block. The good thing about halfway was that my return trip made it a full block. At first, my balance was off and my hips hurt, but I just kept pushing. While all of this was going on, I would take in the nature around me. I remember something my mom said when she was sick: "Appreciate every day because you will never pass this way again." That was very wise and couldn't be any truer.

I walked about six tenths of a mile each day and lived what little I had of my life to the fullest. My neighbor saw me and commented on how well I was doing, and he asked if I would mind walking with his wife. She'd had surgery and needed some exercise. Of course, I happily agreed. I have known them for over 50 years and have seen their kids grow up and have their own families. So off we went. I eventually got my neighbor to walk the same distance I did, and we would stroll along chatting about everything. It was good to see her and have her company, and she started pushing her limits and we would walk even further. Finally, we got up to 0.8 miles.

In May, I realized that walking and weightlifting wasn't enough. I had gotten an invite for a 25-minute stretching session at a newly opened gym. It was called Stretch Lab, and the owner and the stretchologists were the best. When I started, I couldn't bend over, twist, cross my legs, or stretch without cramping up. They worked on me slowly, and before I knew it, I became more mobile and flexible. I have been going there ever since. I can tie my shoes, bend over, sit up, and do push-ups. I still go there every Saturday. The people there are not only my therapists, but my friends. If you want to feel younger, move more, and eat less, I highly recommend it.

By the end of September, I started going out socially. A couple of hours each time. I would take an Uber or get a ride from whomever I was going out with that night, and I even celebrated with my ex-fiancée. That was nice and weird at the same time. We just spoke about everything else but our lives, which was a relief but also awkward. That year, I spent Thanksgiving alone. I cooked, did all my shopping via the web, and made turkey, my mom's stuffing, mashed potatoes, and green beans. Oh, let's not forget the gravy and pumpkin pie! I would sit on my walker and take little breaks to rest my legs. Dinner came out great, or at least better than the hospital food.

At the beginning of December, I agreed to host a high school student from Greece. He was on a basketball scholarship and played at a local high school. It was nice having noise in the house and someone to talk to. We would have dinner together, and I'd help him with his homework and take him to practices and games. He was a really good basketball player, and I enjoyed watching the games. I also made a lot of friends among the players' families. It was something to look forward to, although I did have to endure my fatigue and nausea. At least I was out and about.

For Christmas, I actually decorated and put up a healthy-looking tree. Paris (my charge) helped get the tree and decorate, and as a surprise, I arranged for his brother to visit. He stayed for ten days. His brother had just gone back home when his mother and sister wanted to come for his birthday. They were here from January to February, and it was a pleasure to host them and eat together. Especially since I didn't have to cook. His mom and sister were really nice, and it was great to experience another culture. Paris eventually graduated and went back to Greece, but we keep in touch via social media, and every once in a while, I see him playing college ball. I wish him all the luck in the world.

I have a long-time friend, and I have known him and his family for over 30 years. Once my dad passed, they adopted me. They would make sure I was okay, and we had a tradition of spending Christmas Eve together. For those of you who don't know, that is a big holiday for Italians. I actually got up the nerve to visit him, and it was great to reignite the tradition. I took an Uber, and at some point during my trip to get there, I suddenly realized why older folks carry bags with handles—they help with balance while walking. I just had to make sure I stayed steady. It was nice to see everyone. The food was great (and too much), and it was such a delight to see his parents and the boys (now fully grown). Let's not forget the dogs! Being alone makes you forget what it's like to have family around.

Just to refresh. In my saga thus far, I had gotten engaged; caught COVID; was hospitalized for seven months; was in a coma for four months; died twice; had a stroke, a tracheotomy, blood clots in my lungs and legs, pneumonia, and an abscess; had a pressure wound, an infection, and a feeding tube; lost 80 pounds; got a chronic UTI; had ten months of therapy and ten months to heal the pressure wound; lost my fiancée; got sued by my creditors; lost my job; got a new job; went back to the hospital for catheterization; cured my infection; filed for bankruptcy; learned to walk with a cane and to climb stairs.

I was starting to feel like Joe Pesci in *My Cousin Vinny*, buried under chaos—"Pigs, whistles, trains, sleep! How much worse can it get? And then, in walks the toughest case in the history of murder cases. And you're really runnin' on fumes." My troubles seemed just as numerous, and on top of that I had an ex-fiancée reminding me of the reason she had ended our relationship and considered it all a waste of her time. How much more could life throw at me?

My last milestone was to drive again. I had a second car, a silver 2011 Cadillac DTS. It was the last year of the big Cadillacs, and it could best be described as a land yacht. I hadn't had it serviced or inspected in over a year. First things first, I had to get it started. I called my car club who had no trouble in that regard, however—always a however—I had to drive it about 50 miles before I could get it inspected (modern cars and their electrical issues, oh boy!). Of course, I couldn't drive it because I didn't know how my legs and feet would react. Back to rehab for coordination testing and the dreaded road test. Rehab went well, and my legs and feet were working acceptably. First hurdle completed.

Next was coordination testing. I have had many jobs growing up including limo and truck driving, so I knew the rules of the road and how to drive. Thank God none of that was affected. I aced the second hurdle, and when it was time for the driving test, I sailed right through. The examiner told me she didn't have to apply the secondary brake even once. I was really free! No more inconveniently waiting for Uber or the associated expenses. I could come and go as I pleased.

The only thing left to do was get my car inspected and I would be on the road again! I drove my car to a gas station (aka, service center) to get it inspected. I was so afraid of getting busted because my car wasn't inspected, and I could get a citation. In New Jersey, uninspected vehicles are ripe for the picking, and it is a cash cow for the police department. But off I went—both hands on the wheel, always using my signals, head on a swivel, and slow as could be. I kept thinking that I had turned into one of those old folks who drive really slowly. I justified it by imagining I was trying to evade the cops, driving the same way I would as when I was young after a couple of beers. That drive took forever. Well, it felt like forever, but in reality, it was only ten minutes.

Now, I was truly free!

I was required to have a disabled parking tag, and that took about six weeks to receive. I grew up thinking that parking tags were only for those who drove slowly, held up traffic, and couldn't walk, and I wrestled with keeping the tag on my mirror. It was like a badge of dishonor. For a while, I would hang it and take it off after parking. The stigma of being handicapped rattled through my head. But I slowly realized that it is what it is, and I am what I am.

After accepting that I was a member of the hang-tag club, I started seeing people completely abusing them. Even worse was when they were perfectly mobile and parked in handicap spots without tags. People are so inconsiderate these days. Even while wearing a brace and sporting a limp, nobody cuts me a break, and healthy people use other people's tags just so they can get better parking. Unbelievable!

While all of this was going on, I was working on complicated global products about 50 hours per week. My team stretched from California to Singapore via the Czech Republic. I had meetings at all times of the day and made myself available for whatever was needed. I think I was possessed. With my brain working differently, everything was a lot easier. It is good to be productive!

It seemed that I finally had my life back. I was roughly 80% recovered from my knees up and about 50% from the knees down. Apparently, one of the effects of being in a coma is neurological damage. Your body starts to withdraw the blood from your extremities to protect your brain and heart, which creates nerve damage. On average, a nerve regenerates one mm per day. My neurologist indicated that the longer nerves (in your lower legs and hands) usually get affected, and it was no different with me. He estimated that it would take at least three years to recover, if at all. So much for dancing and playing the drums! I still have issues with simple things, like picking something up. Balance is a problem. One time, I bent to pick something up and somersaulted straight into a laundry basket. Still, there was more work to be done. I guess from all the activity, I developed breathing difficulties. Then it was back to the "ologists". Diagnosis: "Must be COVID." Back to rehab.

This time, my breathing issues were from an inefficient diaphragm on my left side. So, I had more therapy for that, which went really well. However, my blood pressure started to rise, and I had to discontinue my workouts. We tried to figure out the cause and treat it with medication adjustments. In September, I started to feel ill again. Back in the hospital yet again! Well, it turned out that the *infection* came back. Yes, there was that dreaded word again and it seemed inescapable. It was the same infection that I contracted in rehab. I was placed in the hospital with a midline IV. What does that mean? Antibiotic therapy for up to four weeks. I spent the first three days in the hospital just to see how I tolerated the antibiotic. The punchline? I helped develop that very antibiotic when I worked for Big Pharma. I was put in a room with a roamer. I remember the first time I saw him, his entire body tangled in wires with little red lights blinking occasionally. Metal clasps were clipped to his wrists, chest, and ankles, holding the wires in place, and an alarm tower loomed above him, watching him all day and night. I wondered how all those alarms might affect my sleep, and one night, I found out. One evening as I dozed off, and just as sleep began to take hold, one of them rang and beeped, piercing through the quiet of the room—and my ear drums. A time later, when

I thought the racket was over and I would finally get some sleep, another alarm rang. A few hours later, another. And the next day, several more. I got no sleep and had a major anxiety attack. I was up for two days. Then, it was party time, because we were both given Xanax to settle us down.

I was released after three days, but I still had to go to out-patients for infusion therapy every day. And that lasted twenty-three days. On the last day, my infectious disease doctor informed me that I needed to see a nephrologist. Apparently, I was in kidney failure. That was the reason for my rise in blood pressure. I felt horrible and concluded, like Michael Corleone in *The Godfather III*, "Just when I thought I was out, they pull me back in." Ugh, so very frustrating!

As always, everything in my life came at me at the same time. In August, I was informed that the company I was working for was $12 million over budget and my last day would be on September 1st. Just perfect! So, I put my blinders on again—I needed to focus only on my health and recovery. Work through it and get it done!

While all of this was going on, I was looking for new clients as part of my full-time job. After all, I had bills to pay. In addition to everything else, there was health care. Between the doctor visits, insurance costs, medication, therapy, and travel, my costs skyrocketed to about $40,000 per year. I spent all that time looking. I figure I submitted over 150 proposals, applications, or resumes. Nothing. No replies and no interviews. Apparently, I wasn't hirable even with four college degrees, 27 certifications, and 45 years of experience in Big Pharma. It got so bad that I had to borrow money and sell some of my personal belongings just to eat. I felt like I was playing a game of whack-a-mole. Every time I stuck my head up, I got hit!

I found a great nephrologist. He did the standard workup, gave me contacts for a kidney diet and general information, and issued a blood test. Two days later, I got the results. I was in stage four of kidney disease. That's right. Not two, not three, but four. There are five stages of kidney disease leading to kidney failure. This meant that I was one stage away from dialysis. Everything had changed. There was salt, protein, and sugar limitations, and I had to change the entire way I would get nutrition. No more bacon, cheese, bread, or any other good stuff. I couldn't even have a Coke, as it contains too much phosphate. On top of it all, I was constantly fatigued and woke up nauseous every day.

Apparently, our kidneys not only filter waste, but they also control blood pressure, balance fluid levels, produce hormones for the manufacture of blood cells and bone health, regulate key electrolytes—especially potassium which regulates heart function—and affect the acid concentration in our bodies. I guess that is why we have two of them. Redundancy is nature's way of keeping us safe.

I found out that kidney disease is monitored by the amount of creatinine in your blood. It is a measure of the metabolism and your ability to excrete it. The concentration of creatinine is used to calculate kidney function, and this calculation is called estimated glomerular filtration rate or eGFR for short, which is a percentage of your kidney function. Mine was at 20%. At 19%, I would need dialysis and go on the kidney transplant list. The literature I read predicted that, at stage four, my life expectancy was seven years. I never prayed more than I did from that time on. I wondered why God sent me back only to die in this horrible way. I put it out of my mind and just powered through it. *"…I'll lay me down and bleed awhile, then I'll rise and fight again."*

My first question to the doctor was, "Will I get better?" The answer was a terrifying, "No" and "We can only stabilize it and hope for the best." Well, isn't that a kick in the ass! Me being a scientist, I blew through the literature checking for existing therapies, longevity predictions, experimental therapies, and clinical trials. I also wanted to know when this had started. I requested all my records from the three hospitals I had been to. Almost 5,000 pages later, I found out what caused it. That's right, the infection I got in rehab. The bacteria had poisoned my kidneys.

Some of my readings indicated that acupuncture could increase kidney function by ten percent over a three-month period. So, I thought, what the hell, I might as well give it a try. I have been going to acupuncture now for about 15 years. Every Sunday since my diagnosis, I have been getting therapy. Basically, it is needles and electrodes all over my body. I must admit, I look like Pinhead from the *Hellraiser* movies during a session. It's funny because when she puts a pin in my big toe, I feel it in my ear.

Speaking of that bacterial infection, it returned in February and April. Back in the hospital for another three days each time. More IV drugs and side effects. Oh, joy! My infectious disease doctor had a consult with my urologist, and they came up with a plan. After the CAT scans and scoping, we found the problem. By the way, remember when I told you about the removal of my catheter and how bad the pain was? Well, scoping was ten times worse.

I had a stone in my bladder that was harboring the infection, and the surrounding tissue was completely infected. I needed surgery to remove it all ASAP. We scheduled the surgery for the following week, and when the day arrived, it was a same-day procedure with ten weeks of recovery at home.

Same-day surgeries are interesting. No eating after midnight, medications must be stopped some 7 days prior, rides to and from the hospital must be arranged (luckily, my brother came up to help), and a contact must be in place in case something grave happens. The anguish sets in the night before, and you worry yourself to sleep. The next day, it's the same. You get up ultra early, and you are almost comatose thinking about the day to come. In the back of my mind, I was thinking that I already died twice and maybe the third time was the charm. The rest of the day was a fog. I had a full surgery with intubation and heavy sedation.

I woke up groggy, in pain, and attached to a thigh-bag of medical indignity.

And yes, every bit of the surgery was done through my penis. Because why the hell not at this point?

Imagine a Roto-Rooter job—only the pipe is your penis. That's right. Welcome to my life. I tried not to think about how my life sucked, and I just focused on getting better.

Between all of this, I was called back to my old job in May. So, I am working full-time from home and going through all these health issues. I also tested my mental acuity by getting a Certification in AI and Machine Learning from MIT and a Certification in SAFe practices, a framework that helps organizations manage complex projects by improving teamwork, efficiency, and adaptability. I guess I am stronger and smarter than I thought. Nothing wrong with my mental acuity, after all. So, you doctors can take your opinions and stick them in your ears!

I got through the surgery fine. However, I bled for four weeks. I was on antibiotics and my GI system acted up, so there I was walking around with a drain bag and going to the toilet every hour. That thought kept coming back, *Is this the way it is going to be from now on?* Three days later, I had the catheter removed, and I was told not to exercise or lift anything over 20 pounds. The ten weeks flew by, and I healed nicely. I had no infection reoccurrence, and I was peeing like I was twelve (aka, like a firehose). There was some good after all, and I relished it. I saw my nephrologist again and they did another blood test. Wouldn't you know it, there was more good news—my kidney function was now at 29%. I couldn't help but think that God had something to do with that because it was just what I needed—a little bit of hope! So, I just kept going, as usual, but there was no good news without the bad. The CAT scan revealed I had a small mass on my right kidney. Great! My life was mimicking that of Job from the Bible.

I had three MRIs to determine if I should worry or not, and there was an issue concerning the dye causing further injury to my kidneys. The first two MRIs didn't have enough resolution, and eventually they found out that—you guessed it—I needed the dreaded dye. Then it was back to a consult with the surgeon performing the test and my nephrologist, and the plan was to use a low dose of the dye. I prayed and prayed some more! The interesting thing about doctors and hospitals is that they exist outside normal time. There is our time and their time. I got my MRI and didn't hear back for a month, and we are talking about the possibility of cancer! I was finally told my results in November—the test came back with an opaque mass, and I needed yet another surgery. I had two additional consultations, and the surgery was scheduled for the first week in December.

I live alone—no wife or kids, and my brother lives in Florida. I do everything by myself, so that meant another lonely trip to the hospital via Uber. I remember going into preadmission testing, and for all the times I have been to the hospital, they always ask the same questions. Like, "What medications are you taking?" Or "What is your insurance?" As if I haven't told them this a dozen times before. Maybe they think I change insurance plans between waiting rooms. Next came pre-op, and all the associated chaos—changing, gowning, vitals, IVs, and then meeting with the doctors. There was an issue when they tried to decide whether I should be under full anesthesia or placed in "light sleep." That kind of thing never inspires any confidence—trained medical professionals not knowing what to do. I understand that there is often more than one way to go about a procedure, but when it's go time, make a choice and stick to it, you know? Pick a lane and make a decision! Speaking of lanes, there was a traffic jam to get to an operating room. One of the machines broke, and they had to bring in the backup from storage. The surgery was scheduled for 8 a.m. but didn't start until 11. Hospital time sucks!

Here was the procedure—brace yourself! They pushed a hollow needle through my side, guided by a CAT scan. After making contact with the mass, they took a sample and turned up the heat to 240 degrees. The mass was burned out of me, which is called an ablation. I woke up very sore and took an Uber home. But it wasn't over, because that night, all hell broke loose. My temperature spiked to 102, and my oxygen dropped below 90.

CHAPTER SEVEN

On December 7th, I was in the hospital again. I saw five of my doctors and was hospitalized for four days. Blood draws, IVs, X-rays, scans, and testing with everything coming back normal. By the fourth day, my temperature dropped to 98 and my oxygen level was 92, and I was released. I thought the worst was over—yeah, right! The next day, and for the next three weeks, I had a fever of 103. We have all experienced a fever, so I don't have to tell you what that feels like. But as far as the cause, it is basically our immune system trying to defend us from "attack." I also lost 12 pounds and had muscle cramps incessantly during that time. From what the nephrologist said, I deduced that my fever was from the kidney surgery. However, fever also causes sneezing, coughing, and the dreaded mucus. So, I had to deal with that for two additional weeks. I kept telling myself it would get better!

My Christmas and New Year's break was spent in bed. No decorations or celebrations. just rest and a lot of prayer. I started to feel better, and when I went to my nephrologist at the end of January to determine if I had any kidney damage from the surgery, another blood test revealed that my kidney function was up to 32%, and I moved from stage four to stage three kidney disease.

Finally, a break. That had to be God's work.

Just to recap my journey, here is an update: diagnosed with kidney disease, no more wheelchair or transportation services, walked outside with a cane, finished home therapy, pressure wound healed with showers galore, my infection returned with three more visits to the hospital and more antibiotics, had surgery to resolve the infection, convalescence, passed driver's training and started driving again, gained two additional certifications, was rehired by my previous client, diagnosed with a kidney mass, and had kidney surgery and three weeks of fevers followed by slight kidney improvement. I still feel like *My Cousin Vinny*, but it is getting better.

Long COVID is a term that is used to describe the lingering effects of the disease. For me, I have difficulty figuring out what was from COVID versus the coma. Perhaps it was the combination of them both, like a perfect storm. I thank God I didn't develop more serious issues like multiple sclerosis. However, I do have stamina issues, and there is a limit to how much exercise I can take. I often have to pause for a moment before continuing. This doesn't help at the gym when people are waiting to use the machine. All I hear is "Old dude, what are you doing? Hurry up, I'm cooling off!" Just what I need. And what am I going to say, "Hey, I died two years ago—give me a break"? That would not work!

My lung capacity and function have changed, and I have to use a breather every day to exercise my lungs. What a difference compared to before COVID. I used to ride my bike ten miles every weekday and 120 miles on weekends. My stamina is gone now. I used to scuba dive, and my lung capacity was 25 percent above normal. Now, it is just 80 percent.

My pulmonologist told me that is normal, but I know my body, and it definitely is not.

My GI system is a mess. I still have swallowing issues, probably from all the times I was intubated and the scar tissue that developed. No matter when I eat, if I lie down, I get reflux. Even if I lie on a wedge. My digestion takes twice as long, so I have to eat small meals. It is not very enjoyable at all. I never finish a meal, and I get bloated for the rest of the night, so going out is a chore. Socially, it is a disaster. I can just hear it now, "Let's go out to eat." The dread caused by those seemingly innocuous words is quite significant. It means I have to wear my big clothes so I can fit into them when we are done. Essentially, I have to wear pants that can fit two of me in them!

I have general neuralgia. Everything hurts when I sit, stand, lie down, and walk. Because of that, I don't travel well. I am a homebody who must plan adventures limited to short drives in my car around New Jersey. Even sitting on a wooden chair too long hurts like hell. In addition, my balance is off. I kind of meander when I walk. One minute I am walking forward and the next to the side. I even got stopped by the police for being under the influence. That was kind of amusing. The only thing that convinced the officer was a picture of me when I was in the hospital. Imagine this, I am drying off from a shower and I put the towel behind my back to dry off. If I pull the towel too hard one way or the other, I spin around. There are those simple things again!

I come from a talented and creative family. My mom had a wonderful voice and was actually offered a singing contract when she was young. She had to decline it to take care of her family. My dad had rhythm. Music ran through the blood in his veins, and every time something played, he started tapping with anything handy. He was a drummer by heart and he and Mom were ballroom dancers. His nickname was "Jitter Bug." I guess they passed on all that talent to me. I played the drums and anything else rhythmic, and I used to go dancing at the Tavern on the Green in NYC every week. Well, guess what? That's right, all gone. I still tap with my hands like my dad, and I am really good at chair and bed dancing.

I was also diagnosed with Wet Macular Degeneration (WMD for short). Your macula is responsible for your sight. Apparently, fluid has separated the layers of tissue in my eye. What does this mean? Basically, I am going blind in my right eye. The therapy is to get an injection in my eye every ten weeks or so. I have endured a lot of things, but this is beyond me. Sitting in the chair waiting for the injection reminds me of that saying, "Anticipation of death is worse than death itself." And then in goes the needle. Ever get something in your eye that instantly brings tears and pain? This is ten times as bad (even with numbing medication). The treatment takes about two days to recover from, and I have to stay inside during the day to combat the brightness. Needless to say, my prescription changes every year and I am always getting new glasses.

I guess the biggest long-term COVID issue is having a compromised immune system. I have to watch where I go and keep away from crowds, sick kids, and shopping malls. I have even come down with a gluten allergy, which leads to rashes, fatigue, and a myriad of issues that also contribute to my gastric distress. The rashes have to show up on my face, of course, of all places. I can't even hide it. My fatigue is eye-closing, especially when I eat. So, now I am challenged with figuring out a chronic kidney disease diet and a gluten-free diet at the same time. Thank God I work from home where everything can be a little easier. I hope!

Mentally, my life was a rollercoaster. Just a series of ups and downs. I got really good at filing my thoughts and worries in what I refer to as a box. It was a way for me to compartmentalize everything. Put all the bad in the box and lock it away and keep everything I need to get better. I kept thinking, *stick to the plan*. That is my way of dealing with things. I feel if you let sorrow consume you, it is too overwhelming. I needed to take it in little bites to get through it.

However, breaking an engagement is a big one. What intensifies the thoughts is living in the same place where we enjoyed our time together and made plans. I often wondered how my dad did it after my mom died. The heartache of having a companion and someone you loved for 52 years, just gone, and still having to occupy the space you both shared. In a way, we were both the same. We both lived in the same place where the women we loved lived. Everything reminded us of them. My dad was a strong guy, and like he once did, I'm sure I will eventually get used to it. I just have thoughts of all the things we used to do, even simple things like washing dishes together. Those memories still rattle me, but I have to be strong.

A lot has happened over the past three years. I went from being vital and very successful (by my standards) to being physically restricted and financially weak at best. I live my life from paycheck to paycheck. This is not because I don't want to work, no, the opportunities I once had seem to have vanished. I was cast aside, deemed either underqualified or overqualified—whatever that means. The truth is, there is no place for an older, disabled man like me in the workplace anymore. I just try to rebuild and move on. I am alone and will probably stay that way, for I have this fear of being a burden to anyone I may meet, and I have become standoffish. Dating is difficult. It is not what it used to be. Interpersonal skills nowadays are waning. Social media and technology have ruined a good part of life. Funny from someone who makes a living consulting on technology. Going to dinner comprises looking at phones more than the eyes of the person across the table. If I hear someone say one more time that "I am a foodie and have to take a picture," I will scream.

I always had a dog, and I really want one, but what happens if I go before them? Not fair to either of us. So, I visit my friends and their dogs for a puppy fix. Physically, I am a train wreck. I stopped comparing myself to what I was. You know how it goes; comparison is the thief of joy and all that jazz. Cliché, but it's true. My old physicality is gone and will not return, and so is all the joy I got from being physical. For me, it is simply about progress. Trying to get a little better than yesterday. The only good thing about me physically is the human condition. By that, I mean we forget what it's like to wake up without an ache or pain, or not being fatigued from doing little things. We take these things for granted. So, even though I have suffered and continue to do so, I must be grateful for my existence.

Running? Forget it. It takes too much out of me. So does bending down or twisting my body in certain ways. I can fix almost anything, but I can't fix the pain in my neck and back from bending too long, or my hands from using wrenches. But mentally, I am better than I ever was. I have total recall, and I'm much more creative and logical. So, I am just glad I can think clearly and focus. Hooray for little miracles. However, as I said before, emotionally I am a trainwreck. That also shall pass.

Anxiety is an issue now. It never was before. I have been stabbed, mugged, robbed at gunpoint, and have been in car accidents and nothing seemed to bother me. Now, too many hospital procedures, diagnoses, and medications have left their mark. My biggest anxiety is kidney disease and the worry about longevity and all the other organs that can fail. I know I will never get a new kidney (too old) unless I cough up $100,000 to buy one. At best, I will need dialysis. Yes, having money does have its advantages.

They say too much knowledge is a bad thing. My scientific background and my addiction to reading everything I can about my maladies give me pause as to how long I have left. If I get an ache in my back, it could be my heart or my kidney. If I wake up with a blurry eye, it could be that WMD kicking in. If I get a headache, it could it be another stroke. To my dismay, I have become fragile. I am not complaining or scared of dying—I have done it before. I just don't want to linger or be a burden to anyone.

I used to be quite a peacock. I have 30 suits and over 200 ties and hankies, with shoes to match. Even my socks matched. With COVID forcing home isolation and everything I went through, I live in shorts, sweats, and T-shirts now. I guess I am programmed to be like this now. Besides, losing as much weight as I did, nothing fits, and it is really difficult to match compression stockings with my outfits. It may be that my inner peacock is at it, and I am starting to want to look my best again. However, shopping and alterations just seem to be quite a chore. I will have to see if I am up to it.

Currently, my balance and gait are still off. I went back for nerve testing to see if there is any improvement from my first test. Well, as usual, my test came back the same. No change. I was told that if I am lucky, my nerves will eventually regenerate. However, that's at the rate of 1 mm per day. I figure I have another three years to go. I am also seeing a podiatrist (at least it is not another "ologist") and he has me going for PT again. I am glad I am alive, and I will not be defeated. Onward and upward!

As for where I stand now, well, I am alone and that is how it will be. I am at peace with it all. I live my days one day at a time and take everything in. I wake up in the morning in peace, glad I opened my eyes to greet the day. I guess dying shifts your perspective. I am ever grateful, knowing each day brings its own beauty and that I am back for a reason. I get a kick out of people who say their lives suck and that life is hard. Yeah, there will always be wolves at your gate. I guess they don't know what hard is. I can't complain because the thought of where I could have been sets the tone for my outlook. I realize that I was a heartbeat away from permanent disability both mentally and physically. Every night, I say the Rosary and pray for those who have influenced my life, and I thank God for another day and hope I get another. I never thought when I left Catholic school that I would be praying every night. I attend church weekly and take solace in the shared desire for peace among the parishioners. Spiritually, I am good to go!

When you go through something like this, you seek out others who have been there. I sought out other groups just to level-set it all, and to try to find out how their lives have changed and what is to come. An interesting observation has been that if you lived a hard life, you are an old soul who has been around a long time. You are back to being, and by being you assist others in getting through their lives by living yours. How true that is, I am just going to have to see. I have been told by the clergy that I am back for a reason and that the reason will be revealed to me in due time. God works at his own pace, and what he does is for a reason, and His actions influence our lives. My biggest problem is not knowing what or when. My perspective has changed in that I trust everyone. Whether that's good or very bad, I'm still not sure. So, my first reaction is to assist if I can. If I get taken advantage of, I just reset and move on. After all, life is a journey.

I often think of that bright, dimensionless place in my last vision, where people of all backgrounds glowed and walked in harmony. If such a place is where we end up after we go, then every suffering here on earth is worth it. Whatever your religion, beliefs, spirituality, or lack thereof, my takeaway from all my dreams and visions—especially that last one—is that we all end up in the same place if we are good to others and try our best to live a good life. And one day, I know the time will come for me to rest within that blissful light, but that day is not today.